Life Applications from Romans

TS Taylor

All for the Glory of God

Key Verses

"And we know that all things work together for good to those who love God, to those who are the called according to His purpose." (Romans 8:28)

Introduction

Paul's letter to the Church in Rome is filled with deep and sweeping theological concepts. In this devotional, we will look at how to live a Spirit-filled life based on the theological framework that Paul presents. This will be about practical life applications for us today.

TS (Tom) Taylor

Romans 1:1

Why Are You…?

Paul, a bondservant of Jesus Christ, called to be an apostle, separated to the gospel of God…

Paul unashamedly declares that he is the author of this letter to the church in the city of Rome. Even though Paul has not been to Rome yet, he is writing a letter with deep theological content as well as soaring words of encouragement. But before we get into that, we should look a little deeper into the person of Paul. Just who is this dynamic man?

Paul was apparently not a large and imposing man. In fact, his name, Paul, means "small" or "little." However, he was known for having a great mind, as others described his letters as "weighty and powerful" (II Corinthians 10:10).

Paul, known as Saul in his early life, was educated as a Jew, specifically a Pharisee. He was a student in Gamaliel's school. Gamaliel was one of the most educated and respected Jewish scholars of the day. Saul studied extensively the ancestral Jewish law and got an exposure to classical literature, philosophy, and ethics. Saul was so dedicated to his Jewish upbringing that when we first meet him, he is persecuting the early Christian church.

Saul, who was at the stoning death of the first Christian martyr, Stephen, was leading a guerrilla war against the Christians. "As for Saul [Paul], he

1

made havoc of the church, entering every house, and dragging off men and women, committing them to prison" (Acts 8:3).

Saul was heading to Damascus to find any followers of the Way, which was the name for the early Christians, so that he might "bring them bound to Jerusalem" (Acts 9:2). "As he journeyed, he came near Damascus, and suddenly a light shone around him from heaven. Then he fell to the ground, and heard a voice saying to him, 'Saul, Saul, why are you persecuting Me?'" (Acts 9:3-4).

There were many dramatic aspects of Paul's conversion. First, he was a sworn enemy of Jesus and His early church. Second, he was actively pursuing his beliefs and he was persecuting the people of the Way. Most dramatically, Jesus confronted Paul with His Holy Presence. Jesus begins the confrontation with "Why are you...?"

That might be the most important question that Jesus has for all of us. "Why are you...?" As we will see later from Paul's writings, Jesus requires active belief, active faith, and active obedience. Do you need to ask yourself; "Why are you...?

Notes:

Acts 9:6-10, 17

Is It Time for Forgiveness?

⁶ So he [Paul], trembling and astonished, said, "Lord, what do You want me to do?" Then the Lord said to him, "Arise and go into the city, and you will be told what you must do."

⁷ And the men who journeyed with him stood speechless, hearing a voice but seeing no one. ⁸ Then Saul arose from the ground, and when his eyes were opened he saw no one. But they led him by the hand and brought him into Damascus. ⁹ And he was three days without sight, and neither ate nor drank.

Saul [Paul] was confronted by Jesus Himself while he was on the road to Damascus to arrest the Christians there. Jesus tells Paul to complete his journey to Damascus and he will be told what to do next.

Now there was a certain disciple at Damascus named Ananias; and to him the Lord said in a vision, "Ananias." And he said, "Here I am, Lord." (Acts 9:10)

The story then switches to Ananias, a disciple of the Way. Ananias was to pray for Saul [Paul] that he might minister to the Gentiles. Ananias says: "Lord, I have heard from many about this man, how much harm he has done to your saints in Jerusalem. And here he has authority from the

3

chief priests to bind all who call on Your name"
(Acts 9:13-14).

*And Ananias went his way and entered the
house; and laying his hands on him he said,
"Brother Saul, the Lord Jesus, who appeared
to you on the road as you came, has sent me
that you may receive your sight and be filled
with the Holy Spirit."* (Acts 9:17)

Ananias obeyed, he laid his hands on Saul, and
then called him Brother Saul.

One of the most surprising aspects of Paul's life
after his conversion was how he interacted with his
Christian brothers and sisters. Many times, he
probably met a Christian brother or sister and his or
her first thoughts might have been: *This is The Saul
who had my uncle taken off to prison in Jerusalem.
How can I possibly forgive him?* In that same
encounter, Paul might have been thinking: *I
remember her uncle, whom I hauled off to prison.
How can I properly ask for her forgiveness? How
can I forgive myself?*

This is one of the most important aspects of Paul's
personal ministry. He could ask for forgiveness and
he could forgive himself. This is often one of our
biggest stumbling blocks. We cannot ask for
forgiveness, nor can we forgive ourselves. Is it time
for forgiveness in your life?

Notes:

Romans 1:1

The Life of an Apostle

¹Paul, a bondservant of Jesus Christ, called to be an apostle, separated to the gospel of God...

Paul is called to be an apostle, like one of the original twelve. When Jesus told Ananias about Paul's mission, "...he is a chosen vessel of Mine to bear My name before Gentiles, kings, and the children of Israel. For I will show him how many things he must suffer for My name's sake" (Acts 9:6-16), neither Ananias nor Paul had any idea what that meant. Part of it meant that Paul was to travel all over the known world and meet all kinds of people: regular Gentiles, regular Jews, and even some Roman kings. However, Paul's missionary life was not without trials.

Paul reminded the Christians in Corinth of his past and his struggles. Speaking of others, he asked:

²²Are they Hebrews? So am I. Are they Israelites? So am I. Are they the seed of Abraham? So am I. ²³Are they ministers of Christ? —I speak as a fool—I am more: in labors more abundant, in stripes above measure, in prisons more frequently, in deaths often. ²⁴From the Jews five times I received forty stripes minus one. ²⁵Three times I was beaten with rods; once I was stoned; three times I was shipwrecked; a night and a day I have been in the deep; 26 in journeys often, in perils of waters, in perils of robbers, in perils of my own countrymen, in perils of the Gentiles, in perils in the city, in perils in the wilderness, in perils in the sea, in perils among false brethren; 27 in weariness and toil, in sleeplessness often, in hunger and thirst, in fastings often, in cold and nakedness— 28 besides the other things, what comes upon me daily: my deep concern for all the churches. (I Corinthians 11-22-28)

Paul recounts receiving five floggings of thirty-nine lashes. The lashings were always "forty stripes minus one" because it was believed that forty lashes would kill the man. He survived a stoning and three shipwrecks. On one failed voyage he faced one of his greatest fears, being lost at sea.

Besides these horrific events, much of his daily life was filled with perils: cold and sleepless nights and hunger-filled days. In all of this, Paul kept his main concern in sight, the spiritual welfare of all of his churches.

You and I are not called to be an apostle in the same way that Paul was; yet, we are called to Jesus and His Way. Is Jesus asking you to make some hard choices for Him? If so, can you learn from Paul and take some strength from his life lessons?

Notes:

Romans 1:1

Separated to the Gospel of God

¹ Paul, a bondservant of Jesus Christ, called to be an apostle, separated to the gospel of God...

The gospel of God is the good news. In his letter to the Church in Rome, Paul goes into great depth about the gospel: God's sovereignty, justification by faith, and living a Spirit-filled life. Sometimes, before a lesson of great depth, it is good to get a high-level summary. Paul summarized the gospel in his first letter to the Church in Corinth:

³ For I delivered to you first of all that which I also received: that Christ died for our sins according to the Scriptures, ⁴ and that He was buried, and that He rose again the third day according to the Scriptures, ⁵ and that He was seen by Cephas, then by the twelve. ⁶ After that He was seen by over five hundred brethren at once, of whom the greater part remain to the present, but some have fallen asleep. ⁷ After that He was seen by James, then by all the apostles. ⁸ Then last of all He was seen by me also, as by one born out of due time. (I Corinthians 15:3-8)

Paul reminds the early church that Jesus died for our sins, "according to the Scriptures." Paul is of course referring to the many prophetic statements in the Old Testament about the coming Messiah.

He will make our scarlet sins "as white as snow" (Isaiah 1:18). He will come from a virgin mother as Immanuel (Isaiah 7:14). There will be no end to His reign as the Prince of Peace (Isaiah 9:7). Even though we have all gone astray, like lost sheep (Isaiah 53:6), even though our righteousness is like filthy rags (Isaiah 64:6), we will be clothed in His garments of salvation (Isaiah 61:10).

Paul reminds us that Jesus paid the penalty for our sins, He died on the cross, and He rose again on the third day. In this letter to the Church at Corinth, Paul emphasizes the reality of the resurrection. Jesus first appeared to the women, who then told Peter and John about His resurrection. True to His word, He appeared to Peter [Cephas] and then the other apostles. Later, He appeared to a large group of believers so that there would be no doubt about His resurrection. It was not just for the disciples, but for everyone. At the time when this letter was written, many of the five hundred were still alive, so Paul must have been encouraging all: *go talk to them if you have any doubts.*

The resurrection is the keystone event that authenticates the gospel. Can you share this good news with someone? We have all gone astray. Jesus died to pay the penalty for our sin and bring us back into God's flock. We can know this is true because of Jesus' resurrection. Go and share this good news!

Notes:

Romans 1:1-3

Born of the Seed of David

¹ Paul, a bondservant of Jesus Christ, called to be an apostle, separated to the gospel of God ² which He promised before through His prophets in the Holy Scriptures, ³ concerning His Son Jesus Christ our Lord, who was born of the seed of David according to the flesh...

Paul is reminding his Jewish readers of how important the concept of "seed" is. God is always working through His people, through individuals, and through their descendants. The seed is an important concept throughout the Scriptures.

It begins in the Garden of Eden, where God promises the serpent that "...I will put enmity between you and the woman, and between your seed and her Seed; He shall bruise your head, and you shall bruise His heel" (Genesis 3:15). One born of Eve will bruise (crush) the head of the serpent. The story continues many years later when David is selected to be Israel's second king. David proves to be a great warrior, administrator, leader, poet, and musician. At the end of David's life, the Lord promises him, "When your days are fulfilled and you rest with your fathers, I will set up your seed after you, who will come from your body, and I will establish his kingdom. He shall build a house for My name, and I will establish the throne of his kingdom forever" (2 Samuel 7:12-13). Isaiah continues the prophetic message about the Messiah, who will be in the lineage of David:

6 For unto us a Child is born,
Unto us a Son is given;
And the government will be upon His
  shoulder. And His name will be called
Wonderful, Counselor, Mighty God,
Everlasting Father, Prince of Peace.
7 Of the increase of His government and peace
There will be no end, Upon the throne of
  David and over His kingdom, To order it
  and establish it with judgment and justice
From that time forward, even forever.
(Isaiah 9:6-7)

Sometimes the seed comes by a surprising route. For example: Ruth, a Moabite woman, is left a widow and so she travels with her mother-in-law, Naomi, back to Bethlehem. There Ruth marries Boaz. She and Boaz bear the grandfather of David, Obed.

So it is with us. We have a role to play in this life. Sometimes parts of that role are very clear to us in this life. For some of us, the great working out of our role will come from our grandson. God always has great plans for us and for our seed. Therefore, we should always be training those around us "...in the way he should go, and when he is old he will not depart from it" (Proverbs 22:6). Can you help train the future generations?

Notes:

Romans 1:7

To All in Rome

7 To all who are in Rome, beloved of God, called to be saints: Grace to you and peace from God our Father and the Lord Jesus Christ.

Paul is writing this letter to the Church in Rome. Rome is an awfully long way from Israel, so how did this Church get started? In Acts chapter two, Luke describes the coming of the Holy Spirit to the early believers in Jerusalem: "And there were dwelling in Jerusalem Jews, devout men, from every nation under heaven" (Acts 2:5). Many of these different people heard the gospel in their own language and some of these people were "visitors from Rome" (Acts 2:10).

At this time, Peter tells everyone about the person and work of Jesus:

22 "Men of Israel, hear these words: Jesus of Nazareth, a Man attested by God to you by miracles, wonders, and signs which God did through Him in your midst, as you yourselves also know— 23 Him, being delivered by the determined purpose and foreknowledge of God, you have taken by lawless hands, have crucified, and put to death; 24 whom God raised up, having loosed the pains of death, because it was not possible that He should be held by it." (Acts 2:22-24)

Some of the visitors from Rome became believers and took the good news of the gospel of God back to Rome.

Paul describes these early believers as saints. Saints are those called out by God to be His and to do His work. We will hear much more about being called out by God in the rest of this Epistle. But for now, we will rest in Paul's blessing: "Grace to you and peace from God our Father and the Lord Jesus Christ." He is reminding us that we have grace, God's unmerited favor. We are adopted into His family as His children. As such, we have His peace, His shalom. He wants us to always remember that we are beloved of God, and as His saints, we can rest in His grace and peace.

Take some quiet time today to reflect on God's grace and peace for your life.

Notes:

Romans 1:8-9

Faith and Prayers

⁸ First, I thank my God through Jesus Christ for you all, that your faith is spoken of throughout the whole world. ⁹ For God is my witness, whom I serve with my spirit in the gospel of His Son, that without ceasing I make mention of you always in my prayers...

We begin to see the pastoral, shepherd side of Paul here as he addresses the Christians in Rome. While he has not met them, he has heard of their faith. As faith is not something that can be seen directly, Paul must be referring to the working out of their faith. He has probably heard of their great labor in the Lord: caring for the poor and the persecuted, feeding those who are hungry, clothing those who are naked, and proclaiming the gospel of God to all they encounter.

Paul is continually thankful in his prayers for the Christians in Rome. He holds them up to the throne of God "without ceasing."

Paul is giving us two important principles for today. The first is that we should have a faith that is "spoken of throughout the whole world." Remember, these Christians were in the city of Rome, the power center of the Roman empire. Rome required its citizens to acknowledge Caesar as lord. The Christians refused to do this. They knew that Jesus was Lord and that all knees will bow to Him at the end of the age. So it was dangerous for them to proclaim and exhibit their faith; yet they did it so strongly that it was known throughout the whole world. We need to have a living faith like this.

Second, we need to be praying, without ceasing, for others. Especially those who are in the persecuted Church. We need to be lifting them up to the throne of God.

Rejoice always, pray without ceasing, in everything give thanks; for this is the will of God in Christ Jesus for you. (I Thessalonians 5:16-18)

Faith and Prayer; can you remember these?

Notes:

Romans 1:11-12

Encourage Together

11 For I long to see you, that I may impart to you some spiritual gift, so that you may be established— 12 that is, that I may be encouraged together with you by the mutual faith both of you and me.

Paul continues his pastoral tone with the Christians in Rome. He longs to see them, he longs to give them some spiritual gift, and most important, he desires mutual encouragement.

We often think that encouragement is a one-way street, that we are called to encourage the other person. These early Christians knew better. They knew that the Hebrew root of the word encouragement was: to strengthen, to harden, and to be courageous. Encouragement is needed when one of us or all of us is under attack. We feel afraid, we feel that we are going to crumble; we need courage, but it is lacking. We want to give up. Paul's Jewish readers would have remembered wisdom from Solomon:

9 Two are better than one,
Because they have a good reward for their
*   labor.*
10 For if they fall, one will lift up his companion.
But woe to him who is alone when he falls,
For he has no one to help him up.

*¹¹ Again, if two lie down together, they will keep
    warm;*
But how can one be warm alone?
*¹² Though one may be overpowered by
    another, two can withstand him.*
And a threefold cord is not quickly broken.
    (Ecclesiastes 4:9-12)

Paul is reminding his readers that we need each other. Two of us together are much better off than one of us alone. When we are together, if one of us falls, the other can pick him up. We can keep each other warm, physically, and emotionally. In community, we are almost unstoppable, as a threefold cord is not quickly broken.

As Isaiah reminded God's people:

Fear not, for I am with you;
Be not dismayed, for I am your God.
I will strengthen you,
Yes, I will help you,
*I will uphold you with My righteous right
    hand.* (Isaiah 41:10)

Can you reach out to someone today and give that person encouragement? You will find that you will be encouraged together.

Notes:

Romans 1:16-17

The Power of God

16 For I am not ashamed of the gospel of Christ, for it is the power of God to salvation for everyone who believes, for the Jew first and also for the Greek. 17 For in it the righteousness of God is revealed from faith to faith; as it is written, "The just shall live by faith."

Paul begins his discussion on the gospel of Christ by saying first that he is not ashamed of it, for it is really good news. As it was in Paul's day; people today are still ashamed of God's good news, largely because they do not understand it. Many people think it is a lengthy set of rules that are impossible to follow, and these rules take all of the fun out of life. Paul is going to argue that nothing could be further from the truth.

First, the gospel of Christ is power. The word that Paul uses is the same word from which we get the word dynamite. This is a real life-transforming power, so much greater than our own power; in fact, it is much greater than even the power of Rome, the most powerful nation at that time. For those of us who have not been able to change our own life direction or our heart on our own, this is good news.

Next, the good news is for everyone: Jews and also for the Gentiles, including Greeks and Romans. This is very surprising to many of the citizens of

Rome. Jesus was Jewish. He was born of the tribe of Judah, and from the lineage of David. He was born in a small Jewish town, Bethlehem. He spent most of His life in another small Jewish town, Nazareth. He spent very little time with the Gentiles. His inner circle of men was all Jews. He did most of His teaching in Jewish synagogues. Jesus said that His ministry focus was for the Jews: "I was not sent except to the lost sheep of the house of Israel" (Matthew 15:24). Yet, He showed His love for the Canaanite (Gentile) woman and granted her desire: "'...great is your faith! Let it be to you as you desire.' And her daughter was healed from that very hour" (Mathew 15:28).

Paul's message was simple: a right standing with God, righteousness, does not come from doing; rather, it comes from faith. In this case, faith means personal trust. It is allowing Christ to come into your life and to take residence on the throne of your heart. Paul is going to expand on this throughout his letter, but for now it is simple. Real power for you comes from faith (trust) in God. What do you think about that?

Notes:

Romans 1:18-23

What May Be Known of God

18 For the wrath of God is revealed from heaven against all ungodliness and unrighteousness of men, who suppress the truth in unrighteousness, 19 because what may be known of God is manifest in them, for God has shown it to them. 20 For since the creation of the world His invisible attributes are clearly seen, being understood by the things that are made, even His eternal power and Godhead, so that they are without excuse, 21 because, although they knew God, they did not glorify Him as God, nor were thankful, but became futile in their thoughts, and their foolish hearts were darkened. 22 Professing to be wise, they became fools, 23 and changed the glory of the incorruptible God into an image made like corruptible man—and birds and four-footed animals and creeping things.

Paul jumps right into two key questions: "Does God really exist? Can we know that He exists?" He not only says that God exists, but that He has made it known to everyone, all of us. Paul makes it clear that this general revelation does not tell us everything there is to know about God, but it tells us enough.

God uses His physical and visible creation to show some of His invisible attributes. Through His creation, we get a glimpse of His power and majesty. When we look at a starry night or a beautiful sunset we get a sense of His majestic power. When we see a brilliantly-colored butterfly, we see His artistic ability.

When we look at His creation, we realize there are only three choices for its existence:

1. It has existed for all time.
2. It created itself out of nothing.
3. Someone created it.

We know that number 1 cannot be true as we see things, creatures, and people, dying all of the time. Number 2 makes no sense because if there was ever nothing (no thing), there could not be something now, for out of nothing, nothing comes. God allows us to see His creative power so that we might know that He is the Creator.

But instead of acknowledging his existence, we darken our hearts. We make up all kinds of other things or creatures to be our gods. Today our gods are not birds or four-footed animals, but they are immaterial things, such as power, status, wealth, or influence. Sometimes our gods are people of power or influence, such as movie, music, or sports stars.

Paul makes it clear that if we darken our hearts to the fact that God exists, we become fools. How dark or light is your heart today?

Notes:

Romans 1:24-27

God Gave Them Up

24 Therefore God also gave them up to uncleanness, in the lusts of their hearts, to dishonor their bodies among themselves, 25 who exchanged the truth of God for the lie, and worshiped and served the creature rather than the Creator, who is blessed forever. Amen.

26 For this reason God gave them up to vile passions. For even their women exchanged the natural use for what is against nature. 27 Likewise also the men, leaving the natural use of the woman, burned in their lust for one another, men with men committing what is shameful, and receiving in themselves the penalty of their error which was due.

We think we have it all figured out. We think that we understand the balance of justice and personal freedom. We think that we would all be better off if we all just "did our own thing." Unfortunately, when we darken our hearts, when we do not acknowledge God's existence, majesty, and power, God gives us over to our own desires. He allows us to follow the lusts of our own hearts. He gives us up!

Paul is of course referring to Genesis where God declares: "Therefore a man shall leave his father and mother and be joined to his wife, and they shall become one flesh. And they were both naked, the man and his wife, and were not ashamed" (Genesis 2:24-25). We see God's blessing on a marriage between a man and a woman where they come together to love one another and are not ashamed to be totally exposed to one another.

How does Paul describe us when our hearts are darkened, and God gives us up to our desires? He describes us as giving in to the lusts of the heart. We give in to very intense cravings and longing. We give in to our unbridled hearts. We become unglued. He goes on to describe us as giving in to our vile passions. Vile is such a strong word; we use it to describe someone who is extremely unpleasant, disgusting, offensive, or repulsive. Here Paul is describing our unbridled hearts as disgusting, offensive, and repulsive.

While Paul is focusing here on these sexual sins, we will see a bit later that we are all capable of other vile passions. The point Paul is making is that when we allow our heart to become unbridled, when we lose our moral compass, then we are all capable of many different kinds of vile and shameful acts.

When you look deep into your own heart, do you see places where vile passions have taken root?

Notes:

Romans 1:28-32

Filled With All Unrighteousness

28 And even as they did not like to retain God in their knowledge, God gave them over to a debased mind, to do those things which are not fitting; 29 being filled with all unrighteousness, sexual immorality, wickedness, covetousness, maliciousness; full of envy, murder, strife, deceit, evil-mindedness; they are whisperers, 30 backbiters, haters of God, violent, proud, boasters, inventors of evil things, disobedient to parents, 31 undiscerning, untrustworthy, unloving, unforgiving, unmerciful; 32 who, knowing the righteous judgment of God, that those who practice such things are deserving of death, not only do the same but also approve of those who practice them.

Paul is not just describing the sexual sins of which the darkened heart is capable. So that none of us feels too secure in our own self-righteousness, he goes on to describe other unrighteous attitudes of the heart. Paul lists some very unflattering attitudes:

- Covetousness
- Full of envy
- Strife
- Deceit
- Whisperer

- Backbiter
- Proud
- Boaster
- Inventor of evil things
- Untrustworthy
- Unloving
- Unforgiving
- Unmerciful

When you think about people that you do not really like, which of these attitudes do they have? If you could see what they think of you, would you then use any of these attitudes to describe you? Do you need to look deep into your own heart? Do you need to repent of these attitudes?

Notes:

Romans 2:1

Judging Others

¹ Therefore you are inexcusable, O man, whoever you are who judge, for in whatever you judge another you condemn yourself; for you who judge practice the same things.

Judging others is all too easy for many of us. We like judging others, and putting them down, for when we make them feel inferior to us, it makes us feel superior and generally better about ourselves. Many of us have gotten very sophisticated in our judgment of others. We do it in a way that sounds like a compliment, but in reality, it is not. We judge others because:

- They are not always nice, to us or our friends
- They are not very generous with their time or money, especially to the things or causes that we care about
- They get angry easily; they have a quick temper
- They are two-faced hypocrites
- They gossip about us behind our backs
- They are arrogant and boastful
- They do not try to understand the other person's point of view, especially our point of view
- They are slow to show mercy, but they are quick to judge

Paul is saying that God does not need the Ten Commandments to judge us. If He just uses the standard that we use with other people, we would fail miserably. For the standards of niceness, generosity, anger, gossip, arrogance, and understanding that we use on others are too high of a standard for our own behavior. We would not pass the test. God wants perfect people with Him in heaven and even using our own standards we are not perfect. We have no excuse. This is why Paul proclaims, "O wretched man that I am! Who will deliver me from this body of death? I thank God— through Jesus Christ our Lord!" (Romans 7:24-25).

If all of your thoughts about others immediately appeared as a text bubble above your head for all to see, how would you feel? What would others think of you? Do you see what Paul is getting at here? What is your response?

Notes:

Romans 2:3-4

Leads You to Repentance

³ And do you think this, O man, you who judge those practicing such things, and doing the same, that you will escape the judgment of God? ⁴ Or do you despise the riches of His goodness, forbearance, and longsuffering, not knowing that the goodness of God leads you to repentance?

Paul is setting up the idea that there are many of God's standards that we fail to meet. The first is God's standard of absolute perfection, no mistakes at all. This is a non-starter for all of us. However, if He used our own standard, the one we use on other people, we would not escape judgment by even this standard. So, why does God not just strike us all dead and start over with some better people?

Have you ever wondered why God doesn't just wipe out all of the bad people? Not exactly a Noah's flood, but something to get rid of all of the bad people. Of course, how would He decide who is bad: by His standard or by ours? Paul is telling us that even judged by our standard, we would be "bad people."

So, why does God delay His judgment? Isaiah points to His graciousness:

Therefore the Lord will wait, that He may be gracious to you;

And therefore He will be exalted, that He
    may have mercy on you.
*For the L*ORD *is a God of justice;*
Blessed are all those who wait for Him.
    (Isaiah 30:18)

God waits because of His graciousness. Paul points to His goodness, forbearance, and longsuffering. God exhibits these qualities to us, not so that we can continue to rebel, but so we will repent.

God wants us to see His delay of justice, His longsuffering, as an act of grace so that we will repent and turn our hearts fully over to Him. Spend some time today focusing on God's graciousness. Let's see where that takes you?

Notes:

Romans 2:12-15

Our Conscience

12 For as many as have sinned without law will also perish without law, and as many as have sinned in the law will be judged by the law 13 (for not the hearers of the law are just in the sight of God, but the doers of the law will be justified; 14 for when Gentiles, who do not have the law, by nature do the things in the law, these, although not having the law, are a law to themselves, 15 who show the work of the law written in their hearts, their conscience also bearing witness, and between themselves their thoughts accusing or else excusing them)...

Paul continues talking about the law for everyone, Jews and Gentiles: the law that is written on the heart, our conscience.

It seems that throughout most of history the idea of a conscience has been a part of our moral character—the idea of a personal sense of moral conduct, right vs. wrong, that guides our everyday thoughts and actions.

Those outside the community of faith have a hard time explaining the origin of the conscience. For example: Darwin struggled with the idea of the conscience in humans. The conscience seems to go against the idea of the survival of the fittest.

Paul explains the conscience as being the law of God that is written in our hearts. All people, everywhere, seem to have a sense of fair play and they know when the world is not being fair to them. Paul says that the purpose of the conscience is to bear witness to God and His ways.

We see this played out in John's Gospel with the narrative about the woman caught in adultery. She is surrounded by a bunch of men who want to stone her to death. The men know this is a kangaroo court in that her male partner is not brought forward, nor are the two witnesses, who are required for a stoning. Jesus says to them:

So when they continued asking Him, He raised Himself up and said to them, "He who is without sin among you, let him throw a stone at her first." And again He stooped down and wrote on the ground. Then those who heard it, being convicted by their conscience, went out one by one, beginning with the oldest even to the last. And Jesus was left alone, and the woman standing in the midst. (John 8:7-9)

They were convicted by their conscience, the law of God written on their hearts. Sometimes we dampen the voice of our conscience so that we cannot hear God's voice. Do you need to be more attentive to your conscience?

Notes:

Romans 2:17-23

Do You Not Teach Yourself?

17 Indeed you are called a Jew, and rest on the law, and make your boast in God, 18 and know His will, and approve the things that are excellent, being instructed out of the law, 19 and are confident that you yourself are a guide to the blind, a light to those who are in darkness, 20 an instructor of the foolish, a teacher of babes, having the form of knowledge and truth in the law. 21 You, therefore, who teach another, do you not teach yourself? You who preach that a man should not steal, do you steal? 22 You who say, "Do not commit adultery," do you commit adultery? You who abhor idols, do you rob temples? 23 You who make your boast in the law, do you dishonor God through breaking the law?

Paul is addressing the Jews in Rome. They are the religious experts. The Gentiles are new to the religious order and so the Jews are instructing them. The Jews have a long history with God's laws; they think they know Him and His will. But Paul is reminding them that while they know much about God, and they need to be teaching others, they also need to be refreshing their own hearts.

Paul is reminding the Jews of Jesus' strong words as recorded by Matthew:

23 "Woe to you, scribes and Pharisees, hypocrites! For you pay tithe of mint and anise and cummin, and have neglected the weightier matters of the law: justice and mercy and faith. These you ought to have done, without leaving the others undone.

26 Blind Pharisee, first cleanse the inside of the cup and dish, that the outside of them may be clean also." (Matthew 23:23,26)

Jesus calls them blind guides because they are focused entirely on the small matters and are missing the weightier matters of justice, mercy, and faith. Jesus tells them that they are too focused on outward appearances and are missing the matters of the heart. Inside they are full of hypocrisy and lawlessness.

The really difficult part of this message is that, at times, we are all like the Jewish Pharisees. We are so worried about others doing the right thing that we are blind to the fact that we are off track in our own lives. Paul is reminding us all that we need to be continually teaching ourselves. Is there some area in your life where you need to be teaching yourself again?

Notes:

Romans 3:9-18

Are We Better Than They?

⁹ What then? Are we better than they? Not at all. For we have previously charged both Jews and Greeks that they are all under sin.

¹⁰ As it is written:

"There is none righteous, no, not one;
¹¹ There is none who understands;
There is none who seeks after God.
¹² They have all turned aside;
They have together become unprofitable;
There is none who does good, no, not one."
¹³ "Their throat is an open tomb;
With their tongues they have practiced
*   deceit";*
"The poison of asps is under their lips";
¹⁴ "Whose mouth is full of cursing and
*   bitterness."*
¹⁵ "Their feet are swift to shed blood;
¹⁶ Destruction and misery are in their ways;
¹⁷ And the way of peace they have not
*   known."*
¹⁸ "There is no fear of God before their
*   eyes."*

Paul pulls up some writings from the Psalms and Isaiah to remind everyone, both Jews and Gentiles, where they stand with God. These Scriptures are forthright concerning our position with God.

- No one is righteous, no not one.
- Not one of us seeks after God. We have all turned aside.
- Our tongues, throats, and words show our deceit.
- Many that come into our path experience misery and not peace.
- We don't stand before God in respectful submission as we should.

It does not make any difference if we are rich or poor, young or old, tall or short; all of us have a gaping need for God. So, when you interact with your neighbors and find them angry, despondent, miserable, or lost, they may be experiencing what it means to be away from God and to be on their own. Perhaps they are crying out for someone to love them, understand them, and show them the joy that comes from knowing God.

Tune your heart to listen more to these cries for help. Your neighbors may be ready to hear about the way of inner peace. Can you share that with them?

Notes:

Romans 3:21-26

Justified Freely by His Grace

[21] But now the righteousness of God apart from the law is revealed, being witnessed by the Law and the Prophets, [22] even the righteousness of God, through faith in Jesus Christ, to all and on all who believe. For there is no difference; [23] for all have sinned and fall short of the glory of God, [24] being justified freely by His grace through the redemption that is in Christ Jesus, [25] whom God set forth as a propitiation by His blood, through faith, to demonstrate His righteousness, because in His forbearance God had passed over the sins that were previously committed, [26] to demonstrate at the present time His righteousness, that He might be just and the justifier of the one who has faith in Jesus.

Paul begins to clearly present the solution for all of us who are not righteous. Paul shows us that we are condemned by God's law as well as our own standard of right and wrong. There is no way that we can be good enough to meet God's righteous standard. As we are, heaven's gate is barred to us. But there is a way.

Paul says that we can place our faith, our personal trust, in Jesus Christ. We have all sinned and fallen short of the glory of God, but we can ask for forgiveness for our sins. Jesus can take our sins and pay the penalty for our sins as a propitiation. His death on the cross is a propitiation, an act of paying the penalty and making peace. Paul has made this simple enough so that we can explain it to anyone, young or old.

- We have all gone our own way like lost sheep.
- We have offended God with our continual selfish attitudes and actions.
- Jesus came to Earth as a human baby to live a perfect life.
- He then died on the cross, taking our sins on Himself and paying the death penalty for us.
- We need to accept Jesus' death for us by placing our personal trust, faith in Him.
- We will then be at peace with God and Jesus will show us how to love.

Can you explain this to someone today?

If you need a helpful prayer, you will find one at the end of this book.

Notes:

Romans 5:1-2

We Have Peace, Access, and Hope

¹ Therefore, having been justified by faith, we have peace with God through our Lord Jesus Christ, ² through whom also we have access by faith into this grace in which we stand, and rejoice in hope of the glory of God.

Everybody wants peace. We want world peace. We want peace in our communities, and we want peace within our own families. We also want peace within ourselves. We are tired of our own inner turmoil and we want it to stop. Unfortunately, often we will not admit that we cannot have any peace at all until we have peace with God, because peace flows down from the top. It all starts with peace with God and then and only then can we have peace within ourselves. Once we are forgiven, then we can be washed clean, and then we can truly forgive ourselves. Then we can have peace with others. Again, peace with God the Father comes through our personal trusting relationship with Jesus His Son.

Through our personal relationship with Jesus, we can have full access to God's grace. Access into God's grace is access to His full richness. This includes His strength, wisdom, mercy, forgiveness, and love. By His grace we can wake up each day with our hearts filled with peace, hope, and joy.

From His grace, we can rejoice in the hope of the glory of God. Hope is the assurance of things not totally revealed. Some of God's glory we see and partake of now and the rest of His glory we will see when we get to heaven.

With this peace with God, access to His grace, and hope in His salvation we get the assurance of His promises to us. We get full confidence in His daily saving power. We get perseverance and patience to overcome difficulties. We get the indwelling of the Holy Spirit, who is transforming our hearts and minds each day.

You might see someone today who is at war with himself and everyone else around him. If so, can you sit with him and ask to hear his story? Can you listen to his inner conflict and his lack of peace? After listening, can you share your own story of peace and hope?

Notes:

Romans 5:1-5

Glory in Tribulations

¹ Therefore, having been justified by faith, we have peace with God through our Lord Jesus Christ, ² through whom also we have access by faith into this grace in which we stand, and rejoice in hope of the glory of God. ³ And not only that, but we also glory in tribulations, knowing that tribulation produces perseverance; ⁴ and perseverance, character; and character, hope. ⁵ Now hope does not disappoint, because the love of God has been poured out in our hearts by the Holy Spirit who was given to us.

There are many passages in the Bible that talk about suffering. Early on in Jesus' ministry, He told his followers that they would be persecuted. It was always "when" and not "if."

Here Paul talks about tribulations. Tribulations are any trials, hardships, or life events that cause great trouble or suffering. Tribulations have a purpose. They produce perseverance. Perseverance is the ability to keep going despite difficulties or severe opposition. Perseverance means that we do not give up too easily or quickly, but we keep striving towards the goal even though we are being thwarted. Perseverance is something that we must learn; it does not come naturally to us.

From suffering and perseverance, we develop character. Character is developed on the inside, in our hearts and minds. Character is a solid, unwavering personality that keeps us moving towards the goal. As our character develops, we see that we have more and more love, joy, peace, patience, and self-control. God uses tribulations to help develop these character traits in our souls.

Paul then goes on to say that these severe tribulations produce hope in us. Those outside the community of faith, without God, cannot see any good in tribulation. They can only see darkness down the great tunnel of tribulation. Despair is their only companion. However, if the love of God has been poured into our hearts by the Holy Spirit, we can know that God is sovereign over all and that He is in charge. While a particular tribulation may not make sense to us, we can know for certain that God is using it to shape us. Much as a sculptor removes unwanted rock from the granite block to reveal the heroic figure within, God uses tribulation to chip away the unwanted parts of our personality to develop our true character.

When you are in the midst of a great tribulation, can you practice holding tight onto God's greater purposes: perseverance, character, and hope?

Notes:

Romans 5:8-11

Reconciled Enemies

8 But God demonstrates His own love toward us, in that while we were still sinners, Christ died for us. 9 Much more then, having now been justified by His blood, we shall be saved from wrath through Him. 10 For if when we were enemies we were reconciled to God through the death of His Son, much more, having been reconciled, we shall be saved by His life. 11 And not only that, but we also rejoice in God through our Lord Jesus Christ, through whom we have now received the reconciliation.

Paul is certainly not very complimentary when he describes us as "sinners" and "enemies." The Greek word translated as "sin" means "to miss the mark." Enemy is an even worse description in that an enemy is one who is actively hostile to someone else.

We often think of ourselves as just apathetic towards God. We do not think about Him most of the time. We do not invite Him into our lives. We do not seek His wisdom. From God's perspective, He calls this open hostility. He is the Creator of all that is, and He loves us with a love beyond what we can imagine. He wants to reconcile us back to Himself. He has provided a way for this reconciliation. We are reconciled through the death of His Son. Yet, we turn our back on Him.

Paul is trying to make it very clear that this reconciliation is initiated by God, because of His love for us that is shown by God the Father through the Son, the Lord Jesus Christ. So, what is our role in this reconciliation?

We are God's enemies. We are actively hostile to Him. We do not love Him with our whole heart. We do not seek His wisdom. We do not lean on His strength in times of trouble. We actively mock His majesty by making our own gods and idols. Typically, these idols are people of great social influence, not necessarily people filled with God's love, justice, or mercy.

At the table of reconciliation, we do not just have our backs turned to the table, but we have pushed away from the table, and we are running away.

Do you find yourself running away from God? Is it time to look back at the demonstration of His love for you? Is it time to be reconciled?

Notes:

Romans 5:12-17,21

Grace of One Man

12 Therefore, just as through one man sin entered the world, and death through sin, and thus death spread to all men, because all sinned— 13 (For until the law sin was in the world, but sin is not imputed when there is no law. 14 Nevertheless death reigned from Adam to Moses, even over those who had not sinned according to the likeness of the transgression of Adam, who is a type of Him who was to come. 15 But the free gift is not like the offense. For if by the one man's offense many died, much more the grace of God and the gift by the grace of the one Man, Jesus Christ, abounded to many. 16 And the gift is not like that which came through the one who sinned. For the judgment which came from one offense resulted in condemnation, but the free gift which came from many offenses resulted in justification. 17 For if by the one man's offense death reigned through the one, much more those who receive abundance of grace and of the gift of righteousness will reign in life through the One, Jesus Christ.)

21 ...so that as sin reigned in death, even so grace might reign through righteousness to eternal life through Jesus Christ our Lord.

Paul is comparing two men. The first is Adam, the first man. The second is Jesus, the perfect God-Man. Adam was the first of us to exercise his free will. He freely chose his way over God's way. This selfishness and stubbornness are now a part of who we all are. It is like it is a part of our DNA. One of the consequences of this selfish view of life is death: death to our bodies and death of our souls.

Jesus was sent to us as a free gift of God, and by the grace of one Man, Jesus, we can be made righteous in God's eyes by accepting this gift.

The comparison of these two men began all the way back in Genesis. God made mankind in His image. He gave us all the ability to think, love, create, and feel joy. He gave us volution, the will to obey God or to disobey and be self-centered. Adam and Eve fell to the temptation brought by the serpent because they wished to be fully like God.

This caused God to curse the serpent and promise that the serpent would forever be in enmity with the woman and that one day her descendent would bruise (crush) his head. That promise was fulfilled with the coming of the Second Adam, Jesus.

That free gift of grace is still available to us. If you have never reached out to accept that free gift for yourself, can you do it right now? There is a helpful prayer at the back of his book.

Notes:

Romans 6:1-4

Outward, Visible Sign

¹What shall we say then? Shall we continue in sin that grace may abound? ² Certainly not! How shall we who died to sin live any longer in it? ³ Or do you not know that as many of us as were baptized into Christ Jesus were baptized into His death? ⁴ Therefore we were buried with Him through baptism into death, that just as Christ was raised from the dead by the glory of the Father, even so we also should walk in newness of life.

God loves using outward, visible signs to teach us inward, spiritual truths. In this case, Paul is talking about new-believers' baptism. Almost all of the Christians in Rome were first-generation Christians. They did not grow up in a Christian home, so the sign of baptism was particularly important to them. This baptism is a symbol of being buried with Christ and then rising to new life through the power of His resurrection. It is a powerful, outward, visible sign of being born again into new life.

Jesus had many outward, visible signs that He used to teach an inward, spiritual truth. For example, in the Gospels, we read about Jesus feeding five thousand people with just five barley loaves and two small fish. He gave thanks for the food and had it distributed to all of the people. After everyone had eaten, they gathered the leftovers and they filled twelve baskets with the fragments of the five barley loaves. Everyone was well fed, happy, and amazed at this magnificent work of God.

Later Jesus went on to explain the inward, spiritual truth. "Then Jesus said to them, 'Most assuredly, I say to you, Moses did not give you the bread from heaven, but My Father gives you the true bread from heaven. For the bread of God is He who comes down from heaven and gives life to the world.' Then they said to Him, 'Lord, give us this bread always.' And Jesus said to them, 'I am the bread of life. He who comes to Me shall never hunger, and he who believes in Me shall never thirst'" (John 6:32-35).

This is all about the true bread from heaven that gives life: Jesus. He is the true bread of God, the bread of life. We will have a never-empty well of love and joy to draw from for. We will find a truly satisfying life: His life for us.

Think back to one of your favorite outward and visible sign stories? Can you grasp more deeply the inward, spiritual truth?

Notes:

Romans 7:15-20, 24-25

For the Good That I Will to Do, I Do Not Do

15 For what I am doing, I do not understand. For what I will to do, that I do not practice; but what I hate, that I do. 16 If, then, I do what I will not to do, I agree with the law that it is good. 17 But now, it is no longer I who do it, but sin that dwells in me. 18 For I know that in me (that is, in my flesh) nothing good dwells; for to will is present with me, but how to perform what is good I do not find. 19 For the good that I will to do, I do not do; but the evil I will not to do, that I practice. 20 Now if I do what I will not to do, it is no longer I who do it, but sin that dwells in me.

24 O wretched man that I am! Who will deliver me from this body of death? 25 I thank God— through Jesus Christ our Lord!

Paul is totally transparent about his own life. He knows what God is asking him to do. He knows what he "ought" to do. Most of the time we all know what we ought to do. It hangs like a big neon sign in front of us directing our path. But like Paul, knowing what we ought to do and doing it are two different things, because we are stuck in the habit of sin.

We see Paul's internal struggle with his own sin. He not only does not do what he ought to do, he does "what I hate."

He acknowledges that, even though he is a Christian, born again as a new creature, filled with the Holy Spirit, he knows that sin still dwells in him. He calls this his old self, or his flesh. The sin that dwells inside him has no interest in doing what he ought to do. He looks inside and sees that sometimes, "how to perform what is good I do not find."

Paul knows that he cannot break out of his old sinful, selfish patterns using his own power. He knows that he needs Jesus to deliver him from this habit of sin.

We should take comfort in the fact that the great apostle Paul struggled with sin. He struggled to break the habit of sin. If Paul struggled with this, how can we be surprised that we also struggle with our own habit of sin? Can you thank God, through Jesus Christ, that He gives us the power to break this habit of sin?

Notes:

Romans 8:1-4

No Condemnation

¹There is therefore now no condemnation to those who are in Christ Jesus, who do not walk according to the flesh, but according to the Spirit. ² For the law of the Spirit of life in Christ Jesus has made me free from the law of sin and death. ³ For what the law could not do in that it was weak through the flesh, God did by sending His own Son in the likeness of sinful flesh, on account of sin: He condemned sin in the flesh, ⁴ that the righteous requirement of the law might be fulfilled in us who do not walk according to the flesh but according to the Spirit.

Paul acknowledges that we all still sin and fall short of the glory of God. We are all still struggling with our old habits of sin. Even though we are not perfect yet, we receive no condemnation. Paul makes it clear that if we are in Christ Jesus, we are not censored, we will not be sentenced in God's court, nor will we be punished by Him when we stand before Him on the last day.

Paul makes it all about how we walk, either according to the flesh or according to the Spirit. Paul uses the expression of "walking according to" to express what occupies our hearts and minds. What is the guiding force in our direction in life? Is it totally self-centered, formed by our habit of sin, or is it being transformed by the indwelling Spirit?

Paul reminds us that many of us are caught up in the law of sin. This law of sin is trying to make ourselves good enough for God through our good works. We look at the law as a way to live and, if we can just do enough good works, God will be happy with our lives and He will accept us. Paul continues to remind us that this law of sin is too weak, as we are corrupted by our flesh or by our old habits of sin and selfishness.

The only way out of this problem is through God's Son who came to Earth in our likeness, yet He did not sin. He remained perfect while living among us. It is His perfect life that He bestows on us at the end of time to guarantee that there is no condemnation.

Can you rejoice in this free gift of grace and live today filled with gratitude that there is no condemnation?

Notes:

Romans 8:11, 14-15, 26

His Spirit Dwells in You

11 But if the Spirit of Him who raised Jesus from the dead dwells in you, He who raised Christ from the dead will also give life to your mortal bodies through His Spirit who dwells in you.

14 For as many as are led by the Spirit of God, these are sons of God. 15 For you did not receive the spirit of bondage again to fear, but you received the Spirit of adoption by whom we cry out, "Abba, Father."

26 Likewise the Spirit also helps in our weaknesses. For we do not know what we should pray for as we ought, but the Spirit Himself makes intercession for us with groanings which cannot be uttered.

How do we live this new life in Christ that Paul talks so much about? Paul talks about the Holy Spirit dwelling in us. What do we know about the Holy Spirit?

First, when Jesus was with His disciples in His last days, He said it was a good thing that He was going away. When He told the disciples that it was to their advantage, they must have been dumbfounded. "Nevertheless I tell you the truth. It is to your advantage that I go away; for if I do not go away, the Helper will not come to you" (John

16:7a). After Jesus left the Earth, He sent the Holy Spirit to be our Helper, our Advocate.

The Holy Spirit is a powerful Helper in that it was through the Holy Spirit that Jesus was raised from the dead. Paul is saying that we have that same resurrection power dwelling within us to help us break our habit of sin.

When the Holy Spirit dwells in us, we are adopted into God's family as His children, His sons and daughters. The Holy Spirit allows us to call God "Abba, Father." This is an expression of pure intimacy, like saying "Daddy."

The last thing that Paul tells us about the Holy Spirit in this section is that He helps us pray. You can count on the fact that when you do not know what or how you should pray the Holy Spirit will pray for you, and intercede for you. You can be sure that the Holy Spirit's intercession for you is perfect, as He dwells in you, and He sits before God the Father.

Can you take some time today and reflect on who the Holy Spirit is and what He can do in your life?

Notes:

Romans 8:28

All Things Work Together for Good

28 And we know that all things work together for good to those who love God, to those who are the called according to His purpose

This promise is one of the most powerful promises in all of the Scriptures. We must remember that this promise was first given to the Christians in Rome. Every day they experienced a very oppressive government. They experienced persecution from both the Romans and the orthodox Jews. Yet, they held on to this promise each and every day.

The same can be true for us today. We can be going through great trials, tribulation, despair, and darkness. But first, to grab on to God's promise there are a few things that are important to remember.

In the modern Church, we often read this verse to say that all things will be easy. Unfortunately, easy is not a part of this promise. In fact, the opposite is more generally true. Over and over again God promises that suffering will be a part of our lives. For example, in Psalm 23 David says:

Yea, though I walk through the valley of the
*   shadow of death,*
I will fear no evil;
For You are with me;
Your rod and Your staff, they comfort me.
*   (Psalm 23:4)*

Even in grim times, God will be with us.

The second important part of this is the timing. God promises that "all things work together for good," but He does not say when. Often when we are walking in the valley of the shadow of death, we look for a quick solution. Sometimes God does that with us. More often He says "not yet," and He rarely tells us when. He uses the hard experience to grow our patience and our character. Usually, we cannot see this until we get to the other side of the valley and look back.

God also makes it clear that this promise is for His children. He calls us "those who love God." We are called according to His purpose. This is where the "good" comes in. God is working all things for His purpose, always. His purposes are always good. Sometimes we get to share in this good with God the Father in this life, and it is glorious. Other times it comes later.

This is one promise that you should etch on your heart. Also etch alongside it the ideas of suffering, the valley of the shadow of death, His timing, and His purpose. Can you take some time today to look back at how God was using all things, some of them difficult, for good in your life?

Notes:

Romans 8:31-39

What Then Shall We Say?

31 What then shall we say to these things? If God is for us, who can be against us? 32 He who did not spare His own Son, but delivered Him up for us all, how shall He not with Him also freely give us all things? 33 Who shall bring a charge against God's elect? It is God who justifies. 34 Who is he who condemns? It is Christ who died, and furthermore is also risen, who is even at the right hand of God, who also makes intercession for us. 35 Who shall separate us from the love of Christ? Shall tribulation, or distress, or persecution, or famine, or nakedness, or peril, or sword? 36 As it is written:

"For Your sake we are killed all day long;
We are accounted as sheep for the
*   slaughter."*

37 Yet in all these things we are more than conquerors through Him who loved us. 38 For I am persuaded that neither death nor life, nor angels nor principalities nor powers, nor things present nor things to come, 39 nor height nor depth, nor any other created thing, shall be able to separate us from the love of God which is in Christ Jesus our Lord.

Paul ends this chapter with a wonderful doxology. He starts with "who can be against us?" Obviously, lots of people can be against us, but who can be against us who matters? Can anyone who is against us be more powerful, wiser, or stronger than God the Father, who is on our side?

God gave up His Son to pay the penalty for our sin. Given that, can we possibly lack anything else when He is able to freely give us all things in Christ Jesus?

Can anything separate us from the love of Christ? No, nothing!

Paul calls us more than conquerors. In the Greek, we are called hyper-conquerors. Given this, is there anything that can defeat us as we go about God's work? Is there any reason for despair? Is there any reason to give up?

This is one piece of Scripture that is worth reading each day as you begin your day.

Will you do that for one week and see how your attitude changes?

Notes:

Romans 12:1-2

The Renewing of Your Mind

¹I beseech you therefore, brethren, by the mercies of God, that you present your bodies a living sacrifice, holy, acceptable to God, which is your reasonable service. ² And do not be conformed to this world, but be transformed by the renewing of your mind, that you may prove what is that good and acceptable and perfect will of God.

After Paul has built his case about all that God has done for us, he begins his teaching on how to live the Christian life. God loves us beyond what we can imagine, and He sent His one and only Son to come and die for our sins, so that we might be reconciled to God—that is, justified, placed in a right relationship with God.

Therefore, Paul asks us to present our bodies as a living sacrifice. Like Jesus said, "He who finds his life will lose it, and he who loses his life for My sake will find it" (Matthew 10:30). We are to give up, sacrifice, lose our lives to God, and then, and only then, will we find real life.

Paul then tells us that this sacrifice will not be easy, as we are in the middle of a large and nasty spiritual war. A part of this war is a battle for our minds. Satan is working extremely hard to get us to conform to the ideas of the world. This battle for the mind is a very subtle battle. Much of the time today the world tells us to be tolerant of the ideas of others. Unfortunately, this tolerance comes with the idea that all views are equally true, that there is no higher, absolute truth. Instead, there are many truths, and all ideas are equally valid. However, Yahweh, the God of Abraham, Isaac, and Jacob, either exists or He doesn't. Both ideas cannot be true; only one can be true.

In today's worldview, all beliefs in various gods are considered equally valid. There is no Lord of lords and King of kings. There is no absolute truth. The world has been teaching this in many different ways for most of our lives and certainly for all of our children's lives.

Paul calls us to come out of our intellectual stupors and have our minds renewed. The renewing of our minds is accomplished by reading God's word, reflecting on His ways, and talking about this with other Christians. We need to have our minds actively engaged in the things of God. When they are, we will begin to see more clearly the acceptable and perfect will of God.

Will you spend some time this week talking with a wise friend about ways that you feel pressured to conform to this world and discuss how your mind might be renewed?

Notes:

Romans 12:3-8

Gifts – Let Us Use Them

3 For I say, through the grace given to me, to everyone who is among you, not to think of himself more highly than he ought to think, but to think soberly, as God has dealt to each one a measure of faith. 4 For as we have many members in one body, but all the members do not have the same function, 5 so we, being many, are one body in Christ, and individually members of one another. 6 Having then gifts differing according to the grace that is given to us, let us use them: if prophecy, let us prophesy in proportion to our faith; 7 or ministry, let us use it in our ministering; he who teaches, in teaching; 8 he who exhorts, in exhortation; he who gives, with liberality; he who leads, with diligence; he who shows mercy, with cheerfulness.

Paul now begins to talk about how we should relate to others. He starts off by saying that we ought not to think of ourselves more highly than we should. This is a problem for many of us. We think too highly of ourselves. Sure, God has given us special gifts and talents, He uniquely made each of us, but He did not uniquely make us to be better, just different.

Paul goes on to compare us to the different parts of the human body, different members. Some of us are eyes, some ears, and a few of us are mouths. Paul then goes on in this section to describe the different spiritual gifts that we might have. It is not so much about the gifts; but about using them. In his letter to the Church in Corinth, he gives a slightly different list of gifts with a slightly different emphasis.

4 There are diversities of gifts, but the same Spirit. 5 There are differences of ministries, but the same Lord. 6 And there are diversities of activities, but it is the same God who works all in all. 7 But the manifestation of the Spirit is given to each one for the profit of all: 8 for to one is given the word of wisdom through the Spirit, to another the word of knowledge through the same Spirit, 9 to another faith by the same Spirit, to another gifts of healings by the same Spirit... (I Corinthians 12:4-9)

The emphasis here is on the diversity of the gifts. We are all different, but it is the same Spirit who gives. Once we understand our main gifts, we then need to figure out how we can use our different gifts to strengthen the Body of Christ, His Church.

Do you need to reevaluate your gifts and your place in the body? Is there a place where you can go to use your gifts more fully? If you are not sure of your gifts, there is a survey link at the back of this book.

Notes:

Romans 12:9

Let Love Be Without Hypocrisy

⁹ Let love be without hypocrisy. Abhor what is evil. Cling to what is good.

One of the biggest complaints by unbelievers about the Christian church is that it is filled with hypocrites. In one sense this is true. The church is indeed filled with hypocrites because the church is filled with sinners. The Pharisees claimed that Jesus did not spend enough time with religious people. Jesus' response was that "those who are well have no need of a physician, but those who are sick [do]" (Matthew 9:12b). Yes, Christian people are sick. They are sick with hypocrisy; however, they are on a path to being conformed more and more to the image of Christ.

Many times people catch us claiming to have a moral standard, but our behavior does not conform to that standard. When that happens to you, you need to immediately repent and ask for forgiveness. Feel free to explain that you are a work in progress and that you will only be perfect when you get to heaven.

Paul goes on to make it even harder; he tells us to abhor what is evil. That is, we are to hate the evil act, but not the evildoer. This is so awfully hard for many of us. We are not particularly good at separating the evil act from the person. After all, don't evil people do evil acts? Yes, but sometimes good people like you and me do evil acts. Jesus tells us to love our enemies:

44 But I say to you, love your enemies, bless those who curse you, do good to those who hate you, and pray for those who spitefully use you and persecute you, 45 that you may be sons of your Father in heaven; for He makes His sun rise on the evil and on the good, and sends rain on the just and on the unjust. 46 For if you love those who love you, what reward have you? Do not even the tax collectors do the same? 47 And if you greet your brethren only, what do you do more than others? Do not even the tax collectors do so? 48 Therefore you shall be perfect, just as your Father in heaven is perfect. (Matthew 5:44-48)

Paul summarizes these two thoughts with "cling to what is good." Stop being a hypocrite. Stop hating the evil person. Let your love be genuine as you cling to what is good. Can you do this today?

Notes:

Romans 12:10-13

Be Kindly Affectionate to One Another

¹⁰ Be kindly affectionate to one another with brotherly love, in honor giving preference to one another; ¹¹ not lagging in diligence, fervent in spirit, serving the Lord; ¹² rejoicing in hope, patient in tribulation, continuing steadfastly in prayer; ¹³ distributing to the needs of the saints, given to hospitality.

Paul starts this section with "be kindly affectionate to one another." What exactly does that mean? Paul goes on to expand on this.

The first aspect of this brotherly love is "in honor giving preference to one another." Paul is describing a genuine, affectionate love for one another. We take delight in each other, and we take delight in honoring the other person. As Paul said earlier, we are not to think of ourselves more highly than we ought. We should always be lifting up the other person.

We are not to be lacking in the spirit of love. We are not to be lazy. Sometimes it takes real work to love others and to honor them. We are to have a passionate intensity in our spirit. We are to be continually active, not passive, in our love.

We are to be rejoicing in hope, patient in tribulation, and continuing steadfast in prayer. Again, Paul reminds us that tribulation will come our way. It is almost guaranteed. When tribulation comes, we are to patiently hold on to the hope within us. We can only do that when we are steadfast in prayer, always placing our cares, concerns, hopes, and dreams before the Father.

When looking out for others, we need to be focused on their needs and we need to be helping them with these needs. We need to be known for being given to hospitality. We need to be generous in our reception of friends and strangers who may become good friends. Hospitable people are friendly people, always ready to give help or to welcome others with a warm and affectionate smile.

Paul has given us a great deal to think about concerning our sincere, non-hypocritical, affectionate love. Are there some areas here where God needs to work on your heart? Feel free to make some notes:

Notes:

Romans 12:14-16

Rejoice With Those Who Rejoice

¹⁴ Bless those who persecute you; bless and do not curse. ¹⁵ Rejoice with those who rejoice, and weep with those who weep. ¹⁶ Be of the same mind toward one another. Do not set your mind on high things, but associate with the humble. Do not be wise in your own opinion.

Paul continues his instructions on how to deal with others. First, he relays Jesus' hard teaching about those who persecute us. We are not to curse them. This means more than just not swearing at them. To curse meant to call down God's justice and destruction on evil. We are not to call the curse of God down on another person, but we are to ask God to bless them. We are to ask God to pour His favor on them. These are hard teachings!

Paul continues to tell us to rejoice with those who rejoice and to weep with those who weep. Sometimes this is quite easy, like when our favorite team wins. We rejoice with all of the other rejoicing fans. It is not so easy to rejoice when someone is rejoicing at our expense. For example, when a co-worker gets promoted into a position that we were hoping and expecting to get. Paul is not instructing us to be insincere in our rejoicing, but to be sincere, as our love is sincere and without hypocrisy.

We are to weep with those who weep. This weeping here is deep mourning, as the Greek word means to wail loudly. This is often difficult for us, for their misfortune may come at an inopportune time for us. We are about to rush off to an important engagement and now we have to stop, put that aside and put our arm around a sister and weep with her. We have no idea how long we will need to be there with her, but we need to put all else aside and be with her in her weeping. We need to just be there with her and hug her and listen to her.

Paul ends this section by admonishing us to associate with the humble, again not to think too highly of ourselves.

Is there someone in your life who is persecuting you? Is there someone who needs someone to rejoice or weep with? Ask God how He would like you to deal with the situation? Can you reach out to that person?

Notes:

Romans 13:1-5

Governing Authorities

¹Let every soul be subject to the governing authorities. For there is no authority except from God, and the authorities that exist are appointed by God. ² Therefore whoever resists the authority resists the ordinance of God, and those who resist will bring judgment on themselves. ³ For rulers are not a terror to good works, but to evil. Do you want to be unafraid of the authority? Do what is good, and you will have praise from the same. ⁴ For he is God's minister to you for good. But if you do evil, be afraid; for he does not bear the sword in vain; for he is God's minister, an avenger to execute wrath on him who practices evil. ⁵ Therefore you must be subject, not only because of wrath but also for conscience' sake

Paul uses some extraordinarily strong language concerning governing authorities. This letter is to the church in Rome, one of the cities where Christians were severely oppressed. Paul says that they must be subject to the governing authorities, period. The reason for this is that God had His hand in establishing all of these authorities. The authorities that exist are appointed by God.

These authorities are not just Caesar, or the King, or the President. These authorities include those in our State, City, and local community. They are authorities in our workplace, our schools, and even our families. Whenever a new authority comes into his or her position, God is never surprised, for he or she is appointed by God. Even though the authorities are appointed by God, that does not mean that they are infallible or perfectly wise. As good as they may be, they are still sinners. The governing authorities are there for several reasons, one of which is to "bear the sword." They are there to implement laws for the good of the people and keep order in the community.

They are not there to bring "terror to good works." Paul encourages the Christians in Rome and all of us to "do what is good." If we consistently do good for society, we will have praise from the governing authorities. Paul says that Christians should be known as model citizens. Why? For the simple reason that because God appointed the authorities, in some way they are His representatives. So, if you do not agree with your governing authority, what options do you have? The most important thing you can do is to pray for your leaders. "Therefore I exhort first of all that supplications, prayers, intercessions, and giving of thanks be made for all men, for kings and all who are in authority…" (I Timothy 2:1-2a).

Can you pray for at least one person in authority, that God would change that person's heart and that he or she would see that he or she sits under God's authority?

Notes:

Acts 4:18-22

Civil Disobedience

¹⁸ *So they called them and commanded them not to speak at all nor teach in the name of Jesus.* ¹⁹ *But Peter and John answered and said to them, "Whether it is right in the sight of God to listen to you more than to God, you judge.* ²⁰ *For we cannot but speak the things which we have seen and heard."* ²¹ *So when they had further threatened them, they let them go, finding no way of punishing them, because of the people, since they all glorified God for what had been done.* ²² *For the man was over forty years old on whom this miracle of healing had been performed.*

Peter and John are in the temple in Jerusalem at the hour of prayer. A lame man comes before Peter asking for alms. Peter says that he does not have any money; instead, he says, "silver and gold I do not have, but what I do have I give you: In the name of Jesus Christ of Nazareth, rise up and walk" (Acts 3:6). Peter uses this as an opportunity to share the good news of the risen Christ.

However, the religious leaders are very unhappy with Peter and John, and they bring them before the Jewish high priest. The religious leaders command them not to speak at all or teach in the name of Jesus. Peter answers that God's direct command supersedes the command of the high priest, and they will go on teaching.

What would Paul think of Peter's declaration? After all, Paul said, "let every soul be subject to the governing authorities" (Romans 13:1). Paul would have been in total agreement with Peter's proclamation, for although in general we are to be subject to the governing authorities, there are two cases where we are allowed to disobey them:

1. If the governing authorities forbid us to do something that God commands, such as gathering for worship.
2. If the governing authorities tell us to do something that God forbids, such as killing unborn babies.

In these two cases, God requires us to disobey the governing authorities. However, the difficulty is in knowing if the civil authorities are in conflict with God's commands. Sometimes it takes a great deal of wisdom.

Ask the Lord for His wisdom in your situation. Is there an area where you need to stand up to your governing authorities? If this is the case, why aren't you standing up in protest?

Notes:

Romans 13:11-14

Put on Christ

11 And do this, knowing the time, that now it is high time to awake out of sleep; for now our salvation is nearer than when we first believed. 12 The night is far spent, the day is at hand. Therefore let us cast off the works of darkness, and let us put on the armor of light. 13 Let us walk properly, as in the day, not in revelry and drunkenness, not in lewdness and lust, not in strife and envy. 14 But put on the Lord Jesus Christ, and make no provision for the flesh, to fulfill its lusts.

Paul gives the Christians in Rome, and us, a strong call to action. Paul exhorts them to, "do this," know the time, "it is high time," and wake out of sleep. Paul is trying to inspire us, and the Roman Christians, to get going, because there is a great deal of God's work to be done.

Paul tells us that the day is at hand, and we should cast off darkness. He tells us to "put on the armor of light" and "put on the Lord Jesus Christ." Putting on Christ is a great summary of what Paul has been telling us.

We are to renew our minds. We must put off the world trying to conform us to its ways.

We are to take an inventory of the spiritual gifts that God has given to each of us, and then we are to use them. That is why God has given us these gifts:

to be used and not allow the world to conform us to its ways.

We are to put aside hypocrisy. We are to have a sincere love for others. We are to have kindly affection for our brothers and sisters in the faith. We are to be there for our brothers and sisters. We are to rejoice with them when they rejoice, and we are to be with them in their mourning.

We are to continue to rejoice in the hope that Christ gives us. This hope will help us to be patient in tribulation. All through our tribulations, we are to be steadfast in prayer.

In Ephesians, Paul tells us to "put on the whole armor of God, that we may be able to stand against the wiles of the devil" (Ephesians 6:10-11). The Ephesians discussion is largely about defense against the devil. Paul's discussion in Romans is largely about being on the offensive. We are to put on the armor of light so that we can walk properly.

Can you take an inventory of your life and see if there are areas where you need to be more active about putting on the armor of light, the Lord Jesus Christ?

Notes:

Romans 14:1-3, 17

Weak and Strong

¹Receive one who is weak in the faith, but not to disputes over doubtful things. ² For one believes he may eat all things, but he who is weak eats only vegetables. ³ Let not him who eats despise him who does not eat, and let not him who does not eat judge him who eats; for God has received him.

¹⁷ ...for the kingdom of God is not eating and drinking, but righteousness and peace and joy in the Holy Spirit.

Paul is addressing a specific issue that he has heard about concerning the Christians in Rome. The problem involves those who are weak in the faith and their actions and attitudes.

The specific example that Paul gives concerns food that is eaten. Some, whom Paul considers weak in the faith, probably new Christians, eat only vegetables. There are others who believe that there are no Biblical restrictions on meat versus vegetables. The meat-eaters are looking back to Genesis, where, after the flood, God tells Noah that "every moving thing that lives shall be food for you" (Genesis 9:3). Later, in Moses' time, there were some restrictions placed on some types of meat, such as pork; but meat was still allowed to be eaten, although it was not required to be eaten.

In Paul's day, there was a great debate among the Christians. *What should we eat? What should we avoid? What about meat that was used in idol sacrifices?* Those who were "weak in the faith" tended to be more legalistic. When things are uncertain, it is easier to develop a set of rules about what is allowed and what is not. Paul was concerned about this attitude because it reflected too strongly back to the Jewish laws as a way to earn your way into God's favor. We cannot earn our way into God's favor by eating the correct foods and avoiding others.

For those who were strong in the faith, it was important that they did not hurt the young Christians by appearing to be too lawless. That is why Paul ends this section with the encouragement to focus on peace and joy in the Holy Spirit.

Is there a place in your life where you are being too legalistic, and do you need to loosen up a bit? Is there a place in your life where you are hurting the faith of others with your loose view? Do you need to consider others and strike a better balance in your life?

Notes:

Romans 15:14-20

Go and Preach

14 Now I myself am confident concerning you, my brethren, that you also are full of goodness, filled with all knowledge, able also to admonish one another. 15 Nevertheless, brethren, I have written more boldly to you on some points, as reminding you, because of the grace given to me by God, 16 that I might be a minister of Jesus Christ to the Gentiles, ministering the gospel of God, that the offering of the Gentiles might be acceptable, sanctified by the Holy Spirit. 17 Therefore I have reason to glory in Christ Jesus in the things which pertain to God. 18 For I will not dare to speak of any of those things which Christ has not accomplished through me, in word and deed, to make the Gentiles obedient— 19 in mighty signs and wonders, by the power of the Spirit of God, so that from Jerusalem and round about to Illyricum I have fully preached the gospel of Christ. 20 And so I have made it my aim to preach the gospel, not where Christ was named, lest I should build on another man's foundation...

In summarizing his letter to the Christians in Rome, Paul is reminding them that he is confident in their faith, as he started the letter with "your faith is spoken of throughout the whole world" (Romans

1:8). He is also reminding them that his mission is to be from Jerusalem to Illyricum. But where is Illyricum?

Paul's mission was generally to the west of Jerusalem. He traveled to places such as Ephesus, Corinth, and Thessalonica. Illyricum is over 400 miles northwest of Thessalonica. Paul was making it clear that he wanted to go to places where Christ was not named, in other words, where the good news of Christ had not been heard.

You might be saying to yourself, *there are not any Illyricum places anymore.* Not true! Your neighborhood may be a place where Christ is not named. It may be a place where, though people have heard the name Jesus Christ, they have no idea what it means. Can you share some of the lessons from Paul's letter to the Romans?

1. Don't be afraid, for the gospel of Christ is the power of God to salvation.
2. They know, deep down in their hearts, that God exists because He has shown it to them.
3. They know that they do not seek after God.
4. They know that, even by their own standards, they are not very good.

You just need to share that God has provided a way back to Him through His Son Jesus. Can you share this good news with someone this week?

Notes:

Romans 15:30-33, 16:1-5

The Saints

30 Now I beg you, brethren, through the Lord Jesus Christ, and through the love of the Spirit, that you strive together with me in prayers to God for me, 31 that I may be delivered from those in Judea who do not believe, and that my service for Jerusalem may be acceptable to the saints, 32 that I may come to you with joy by the will of God, and may be refreshed together with you. 33 Now the God of peace be with you all. Amen.

16 I commend to you Phoebe our sister, who is a servant of the church in Cenchrea, 2 that you may receive her in the Lord in a manner worthy of the saints, and assist her in whatever business she has need of you; for indeed she has been a helper of many and of myself also. 3 Greet Priscilla and Aquila, my fellow workers in Christ Jesus, 4 who risked their own necks for my life, to whom not only I give thanks, but also all the churches of the Gentiles. 5 Likewise greet the church that is in their house. Greet my beloved Epaenetus, who is the firstfruits of Achaia to Christ.

Paul urges the brothers and sisters in Rome to pray with him that his service would be acceptable and that they may be together one day, to be refreshed together.

In his absence, he commends the saints in the fellowship. "Saints" today means you and me, the fellow believers in the fellowship. Paul commends many by name.

Paul commends Phoebe, who was not only a servant, a helper of many, but she was also trusted to deliver the letter to the church in Rome. This was indeed an incredibly special task for a woman in Paul's day.

Priscilla and Aquila were probably Jews expelled from Rome who met up with Paul in Corinth. They ministered with Paul for about 18 months and probably assisted him in his tent-making business. As a husband-and-wife team, they apparently risked their lives for Paul, protecting him and thus allowing the gospel to be spread throughout the world.

Paul mentions Epaenetus as being the first convert from Asia. It is believed that he went on to be the first Bishop of Carthage.

Paul makes it clear that all kinds of people can be fellow laborers with him: men, women, and married couples.

He is encouraging all of us to strive together with him. Are you ready to take your place alongside the apostle Paul?

Notes:

Spiritual Gifts

There are lots of helps and surveys around spiritual gifts. If you have never tested for your unique spiritual gifts, or if it has been a long time since you have done it; do it.

If you need an example, one is below:

https://www.lifeway.com/en/articles/women-leadership-spiritual-gifts-growth-service

If you click on; Spiritual Gifts Survey (Discovery Tool)

You will get a downloaded PDF.

Enjoy the adventure!

Concluding Thoughts

Paul has written a deep and rich letter to the Christians in Rome. It is much more than being about God's righteousness and forgiveness. It is much more than the Law and the Spirit. It is about how to live a Christ-filled life in this world. Drink deeply from Paul's thoughts and go and join him in proclaiming God's good news to your world

Prayer to Accept Jesus

If you found this devotional book helpful and you felt God tugging at your heart, you can respond to the Holy Spirit right now.

If you have never accepted Jesus as your own personal Lord and Savior, you can do that with a simple prayer.

You can pray something like this:

"Thank you, God, for loving me and sending your Son to die for my sins. I sincerely repent of my sins, and receive Christ as my personal savior. Now, as your child, I turn my entire life over to you. Amen."

If you have any questions, you can reach out to me at:

tstaylor-devotionals@gmail.com

May God bless you on your own spiritual journey.

Acknowledgments

I wish to thank my class at the Church of the Apostles in Atlanta, Georgia. They worked through much of this material, as we learned from the Scriptures together.

Thanks to Jane Ledbetter for her great editing work.

Soli Deo Gloria

Made in the USA
Columbia, SC
06 June 2023

17488376R00052